Mindful SPACES

MINDFULNESS AND ME

Written by Dr. Rhianna Watts
and Katie Woolley
Illustrated by Sarah Jennings

First published in the United States by Mayo Clinic Press Kids, an imprint of Mayo Clinic Press. All rights reserved. No part of this publication may be reproduced, stored in a retrieval system, or transmitted, in any form or by any means, electronic, mechanical, photocopying, recording, or otherwise, without the prior written permission of the publisher. Originally published by Wayland, an imprint of Hachette Children's Group UK, London, in 2022.

For bulk sales to employers, member groups and health-related companies, contact Mayo Clinic at SpecialSalesMayoBooks@mayo.edu.

Proceeds from the sale of every book benefit important medical research and education at Mayo Clinic.

First American Edition 2024

MAYO CLINIC PRESS
200 First St. SW
Rochester, MN 55905
mcpress.mayoclinic.org

To stay informed about Mayo Clinic Press, please subscribe to our free e-newsletter at mcpress.mayoclinic.org or follow us on social media.

ISBN: 979-8-887-70127-1 (paperback) | 979-8-887-70130-1 (ebook) | 979-8-887-70116-5 (library binding)

Library of Congress Cataloging-in-Publication Data is available upon request.

MANUFACTURED IN CHINA

SAFETY PRECAUTIONS

We recommend adult supervision at all times while doing the exercises and activities in this book, particularly outdoors, and with activities involving exercise, glue, and scissors. When you are doing creative activities:

- Cover surfaces.
- Tie back long hair.
- Ask an adult for help with cutting.
- Check all ingredients for allergens.

Contents

WHAT IS MINDFULNESS?

Mindfulness is about paying attention to what is going on inside your mind and your body, as well as what is happening in the world around you.

We all lead busy lives and it can be easy to get caught up in our own experiences. By slowing down and paying attention, mindfulness tells you about the present moment. Not what happened five minutes ago, or what may happen five minutes in the future, but what is happening *now*.

Connect to the World

Exercise

Start at the bottom of the mountain and follow these steps to connect to your present moment.

3. Then bend forward as you breathe out, swinging your arms down to the floor and back up again.

2. Breathe in and stretch your arms up above your head, towards the sky.

1. Stand with your feet apart. Feel the weight of your feet on the ground.

HOW THIS EXERCISE HELPS

Your experience changes moment by moment. You can learn to connect with your world by slowing down and paying attention to what stays the same, what changes, and what comes and goes around you.

4. Imagine you are scooping up the things you can see— objects in the room or, if you are outside, things in nature.

5. Then bend forward again and swing your arms to let those things go.

6. Repeat steps 3 to 5 a few times. Do you notice anything new each time you scoop upwards?

WHY IS MINDFULNESS HELPFUL?

Mindfulness can help you better understand your thoughts, emotions, and actions. Slowing down creates a bit of space between what happens to you and how you react. This can allow you to make better decisions and give you more control over how you choose to respond to the world.

This, in turn, can lead to you feeling more confident in your mind, your body, your abilities, and your choices so that you can find some calm in a busy, noisy world.

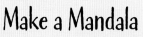

Make a Mandala

A mandala is a circular pattern that represents the beauty of the universe. Try creating your own mandala with this mindful activity.

You will need: a paper circle or plate, glue, and objects that matter to you.
1. Use a circular piece of paper or a paper plate.
2. Ask an adult to help you glue some objects that are important to you onto the paper. The objects might be shells, painted stones, pretty flowers—it's up to you.
3. Place them on the paper in a repeating pattern, working from the outside into the middle.
4. In the center, you could write a positive affirmation (something nice that you think about yourself) to remind you how special you are.
5. Spend a few minutes every day looking at it. Take your time noticing and observing the shapes, colors, and patterns.

HOW THIS ACTIVITY HELPS

Making a mandala is a good activity to practice slowing down. It gives you time to reflect on your experiences and think about what makes you 'you.'

HOW CAN I BE MINDFUL?

The idea of mindfulness seems so simple at first—slow down and pay attention. But this can actually be really hard to do because we often act and react too quickly! Even when we try to slow down and pay attention, our minds can wander and get distracted.

Your mind is a bit like a puppy: you might want your mind to stay focused, like a dog owner who wants their puppy to walk beside them. But your mind might wander off and get caught up in something else, like a puppy running off to explore!

A Sensory Walk

When you next go for a walk, notice the sensations in your body. What can you feel, smell, hear, taste, and see? Is the air warm or cold on your skin? What color is the sky? What can you hear? Birds? Cars? Think about each of your senses as you focus on what is happening in that moment.

HOW THIS EXERCISE HELPS

Paying attention to your five senses helps you connect with what is happening to you right here and now. Your senses and your breath can anchor you to the present moment.

MINDFUL MOMENTS

Here are two moments of mindfulness that helped these kids cope with a challenge. What would you do in these situations?

Abdalla is doing his homework. He's trying to focus, but his mind is racing. He is caught up in thoughts like *"this is too hard."* and, *"I can't do this."* He takes some deep breaths and goes outside to enjoy the sunshine. He can hear birds tweeting and he can smell the flowers. His hands feel cool on the grass. Slowly, his mind begins to settle. His mindful practice has helped to calm his racing thoughts and settle his emotions. Abdalla is ready to try and complete his homework again.

Sienna is playing her favorite game on her tablet. Her family is talking and laughing, but Sienna is too caught up in her game to notice. Grandma asks her to turn the tablet off.

At first, Sienna gets annoyed. Grandma interrupted an important part of the game, but then she remembers her mindfulness. She stops, takes a deep breath, looks around her and pays attention to everything she can see and hear in that moment (not just what is on her tablet.)

She realizes that she is missing out on fun family time. Sienna decides to pause the game and join her family instead. Mindfulness helped Sienna slow down, pay attention to everything going on around her, and make a decision about what to do.

PRACTICE A LITTLE EVERY DAY

Take a few moments every day to slow down and pay attention to the things around you and how your body feels as you go about daily life. For example, when you go for a walk or brush your teeth.

You could also try some more structured mindfulness exercises. Why don't you pick one of these activities and see if you can do it every day for a week?

Mindful eating: Next time you eat something you really like, slow down and enjoy it. Before you eat it, take time to look at it, feel it, and smell it. Then, take a small bite, but don't chew. Let it rest on your tongue for a few moments to see what it feels and tastes like. Next, slowly chew and swallow, noticing what that feels and tastes like.

Mindful dancing: Close your eyes and listen to your favorite music. Then start to dance! Pay attention to how your body feels, notice what emotions and thoughts come up as you dance and let go of any judgements, such as "I feel silly." or "I can't dance." Redirect all of your attention to simply dancing to your favorite tune.

Mindful breathing: Sit on a chair with your feet flat on the floor and your back straight. Notice how your feet feel on the floor. Notice how your body feels on the chair. Take a deep breath in through your nose, pause, and then breathe out slowly through your mouth. Notice how it feels as the air travels in and out. Repeat for a few minutes, giving your breath all of your attention. If your mind wanders, that's okay. Simply bring it back to your breath.

MINDFUL MUSCLES

Mindfulness is a skill and, like all skills, it requires practice. The more you practice, the easier it becomes—a bit like exercising your physical muscles and building muscle memory in your body.

To become skilled at using mindfulness, it can be helpful to practice paying attention.

1. Set aside a regular time to practice every day.

2. Make yourself comfortable – this could be sitting on the floor of your living room or it could be lying down on your bed.

3. Try a few different mindfulness exercises to see which ones you like best. You could try focusing on your breath or any sounds you can hear around you. Stop doing an exercise if it feels uncomfortable.

4. It is important to go slowly, and be patient and kind to yourself. You are learning a new skill and this isn't always easy.

5. Remind yourself it's okay if your mind wanders, that's just what minds do. Notice where your mind has gone and gently guide it back to the exercise, like you would do with a puppy who has run off to explore!

Mindfulness Stones

On a walk, look for some special stones to collect. They could be flat or round, smooth or rough, large or small.

When you get home, paint and decorate some stones and leave others plain, just as they are. You have created your own set of mindfulness stones.

HOW THIS ACTIVITY HELPS

Spending some time being mindful as you create your own set of mindfulness stones helps you focus on the present moment. You can use your stones to help you practice mindfulness every day, by spending a few minutes holding them in your hands and giving them your complete attention. What do they feel, look, and maybe even smell like?

TUNING INTO THE WORLD

You can learn to tune into the world around you by slowing down and paying attention to your senses – what you can see, hear, taste, smell, and touch.

Activity

Make Your Own Musical Shaker

You will need: an adult to help you, an empty plastic bottle, scissors, a balloon, an elastic band, some dried lentils or pasta, and decorations.

1. Fill your bottle with lentils or pasta. How much you put in will affect the sound of your instrument.

2. Ask an adult to cut off the end of your balloon.

3. Place the balloon over one end of your bottle, so that it is stretched tightly across the bottle's opening.

4. Secure it with a rubber band.

5. You can decorate your shaker however you like.

6. Shake your instrument in time to your favorite song.

HOW THIS ACTIVITY HELPS

Paying attention to your senses, such as what you can hear, helps you learn how to focus your mind on one thing at a time as you tune into the world.

TUNING INTO YOUR BODY

You can learn to tune into what is happening in your body by slowing down and focusing your attention on any physical sensations you can feel. Notice how these sensations come and go.

Tree Pose

1. Stand with your feet together and your arms by your side. Keep your back straight and your eyes open.

2. Feel your feet anchor your body to the ground, as though you are growing roots from the soles of your feet into the ground.

3. Slowly lift one foot so that the bottom of it rests on the ankle of your other foot.

4. When you find your balance, raise your hands above your head so your palms are touching.

18

5. Breathe in and out three times, filling your lungs completely each time, before lowering your arms to your sides.

6. Repeat this exercise three times and, as you do, notice the sensations in your body and how they change as your movements change. If you get distracted, simply notice where your mind has gone, and gently guide it back to paying attention to your body.

Remember!

It is important to do mindfulness exercises that feel comfortable. If you notice discomfort in your body, imagine gently breathing into that part of your body and see if that helps. If the discomfort remains, try changing your position. If it doesn't get better, then stop doing the exercise.

HOW THIS EXERCISE HELPS

Practicing focusing your attention on your body's sensations and how it feels as you move, stretch, or balance, helps you learn to focus your mind on one thing at a time.

TUNING INTO YOUR MIND

Learning to pay attention to what you are thinking and feeling is an important part of practicing mindfulness, so that you can welcome your experiences without judging them as good or bad.

You can learn to tune into your mind by slowing down and paying attention to your thoughts and emotions, without getting caught up in them. You can notice them as experiences that come and go—just like physical sensations in your body.

A Mindful Meal

Before you have your breakfast, lunch, or dinner, stop what you are doing for a moment and check in with yourself. What emotions are around right now? What thoughts are going through your head? Try to simply notice and welcome them—you don't need to 'do anything' with these thoughts. Notice if they are the same or different to those before previous meals. Notice how thoughts and emotions come and go. Then refocus on your meal.

Exercise

HOW THIS EXERCISE HELPS

Learning to tune into your mind means you can start to recognize thoughts and emotions as events that come and go, that are in some way separate from you, and to which you can choose how you want to respond.

FINDING GRATITUDE

As you begin to practice mindfulness regularly, you will start to see that you have a new appreciation for the world and your place within it.

By slowing down and noticing your surroundings, you can admire the beauty of it all: the flutter of a butterfly, the warmth of the sun on your skin, and the feeling of laughing with a friend. You can find joy in the way your mind and body responds in the present moment.

Time to read my favorite book

Playing outside

My friends

List of Gratitude

At the end of the day, write a list of the good things that happened. You could draw a picture of all the things you are thankful for, too.

Activity

My family

Sunny days

Yummy food

HOW THIS ACTIVITY HELPS

When you rush through life you often forget to stop and notice good things, which can mean you focus on more upsetting or worrying things as these tend to pull at your attention. By slowing down and paying attention to good things that have happened to you, you can feel happier and more content.

FINDING CONFIDENCE

There will be times in your life when things aren't easy. Your emotions may feel overwhelming and tricky to navigate.

Mindfulness can help you pay attention to your emotions and what they are telling you about the world in that moment. It can help you trust your mind and your body, and trust that the decisions you make on how to act will lead to a positive outcome.

Words of Courage

1. Sit comfortably with your back straight.
2. Think of something you would like to do but haven't felt brave enough to try yet.
3. Instead of worrying about it, imagine a friend is encouraging you.
4. Use those positive words on yourself instead. Let the words seep into your body. How do the words make you feel?
5. Maybe next time you want to do something you feel unsure about, remember these words of courage and see if they help you feel a little bit braver.

HOW THIS EXERCISE HELPS

It can be hard to think good things about yourself. Taking the time to remember what makes you YOU can help you feel more confident in yourself.

25

FINDING CALM

After a busy day at school, it can be hard to stop your mind from whirring. It can be full of the thoughts and experiences of the day.

Reading a book or writing in a journal are good ways to unwind at the end of the day, but you could also take a moment to do a mindfulness exercise, such as coloring, to find a moment of calm in a noisy world.

Finding Calm

You will need: a piece of paper and some color pencils.

1. Think of a setting that makes you feel calm and relaxed. It could be a beach, a nature walk, a library, or even your own bedroom.
2. Draw your calm setting. Don't forget to add yourself into the scene.
3. Color it in with your pencils. Focus on the coloring activity and try not to let your mind wander.
4. If it does wander, that's okay. Try to bring your mind back to the task again.

HOW THIS ACTIVITY HELPS

A creative activity can help you focus your mind on one thing at a time. Spending time being mindful as you color—look at the picture, pay attention to what you can see, imagine yourself there, and notice how your thoughts and emotions settle. This helps your mind get ready to sleep.

MY MINDFUL JOURNEY

Becoming mindful is a journey. By reading this book and beginning to think about mindfulness, you are on the start of your journey. As you practice mindfulness more often in everyday life, you will become more mindful.

Mindfulness Plan

Make a map or a list of how you will keep practicing and using mindfulness to help you feel calm and happy as you move forward into your future.

1. Sit cross-legged and breathe deep

2. Mindful coloring

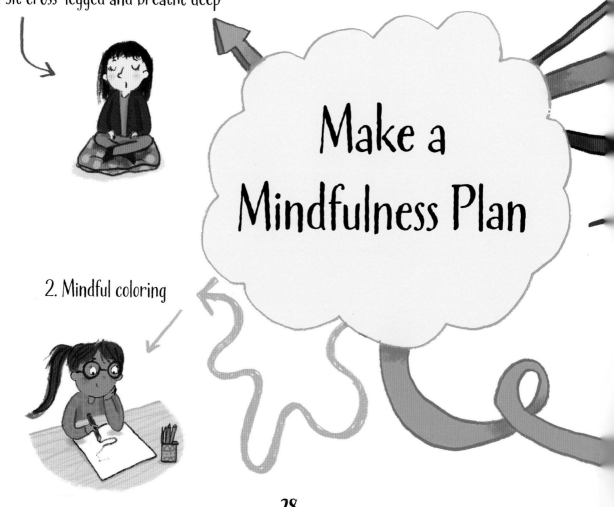

Make a Mindfulness Plan

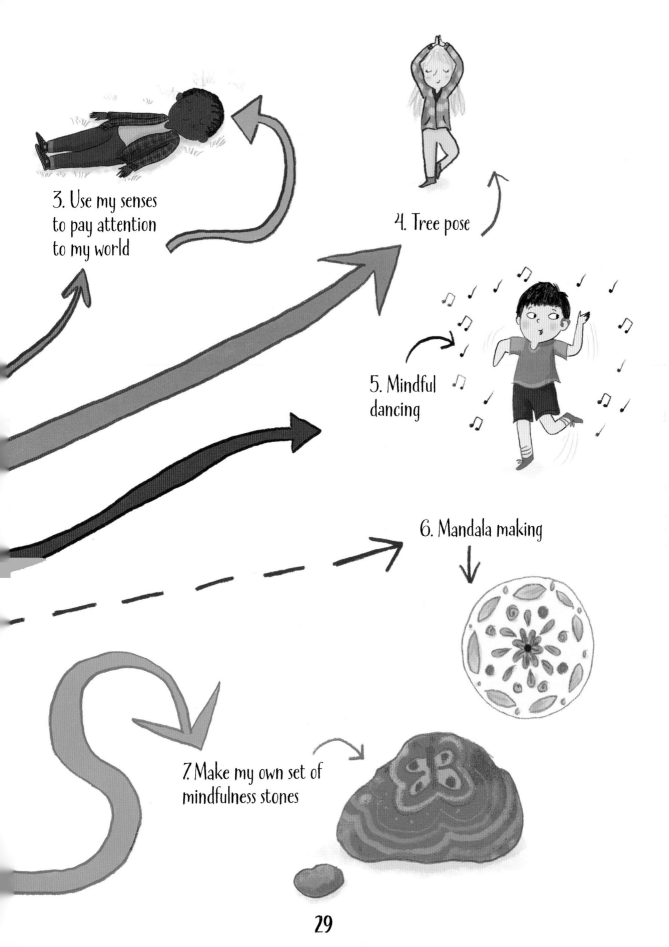

3. Use my senses to pay attention to my world

4. Tree pose

5. Mindful dancing

6. Mandala making

7. Make my own set of mindfulness stones

29

MINDFULNESS TIPS

Mindfulness anchors you in the present moment. It helps you feel confident and ready to tackle the day. It can help you navigate big emotions and it can help you find moments of calm in your busy world.

Here are some tips to help you practice mindfulness:

* You can practice mindfulness anywhere and at any time. Mindfulness simply means choosing to pay attention to what is happening inside your mind and body, and what is happening around you, in the present moment, right here and right now.

* You can do this by sitting and focusing on your breath for five minutes in bed before you go to sleep, or you could do this by focusing on what you can see and hear while walking to school!

* Your breath and how it feels in your body is very important. Paying attention to your breath helps you focus on what is happening in the present moment. Your breath is like an anchor for your mind and body. It can stop them from floating away.

* It's okay if you start to feel a little bored or if your mind wanders. If you can, just notice this and refocus your mind to where you want it to be. If you get stuck, be kind to yourself. Remember you are learning a new skill, and you can always try again another day.

* If your body starts to feel uncomfortable, notice where in your body you feel any aches and move so you are in a more comfortable position. However, always stop doing an exercise if you feel pain.

INDEX

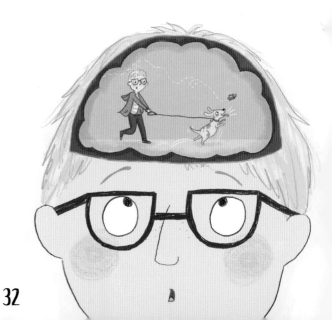